Quick N' Easy Low Carb Cookbook

SIMPLE | DELICIOUS | DIET FRIENDLY

JOHN JACKSON

TABLE OF CONTENTS

SLOW COOKER

BREAD AND BAKING:

Appetizers

Jalapeño Poppers

Ingredients:

8 fresh jalapeños

4 ounces cream cheese, softened

8 slices thin bacon, cut in half crosswise

Directions:

-Cut the chiles in half lengthwise; scrape out seeds and membranes. Fill each half with cream cheese, but do not mound it. Four ounces should be just about the right amount for 8 average size jalapeño halves. If you have extra large chiles, make sure you have a full 8 ounces of cream cheese on hand.

-Wrap each with 1/2 slice raw bacon, making sure to start with the end on the bottom of the chile. Stretch the bacon slightly to make it go all the way around each chile once, then tuck ends underneath.

-Place cream cheese side up on foil-lined baking sheet. These can be assembled and chilled until just before baking and serving.

-Bake at 375º 20-25 minutes. If bacon isn't quite done, broil a few more minutes to brown.

Makes 16 Servings

Per Popper: 45 Calories; 4g Fat; 2g Protein; 1g Carbohydrate; trace Dietary Fiber; .5g Net Carbs

Garlic Cheese Balls

Ingredients:

4 ounces sharp cheddar cheese, shredded

4 onces cream cheese, softened

1/2 teaspoon garlic powder

1/2 teaspoon Worcestershire sauce

Pinch cayenne, optional

1 ounce pecans, coarsely chopped, 1/4 cup

Directions:

-Put the cheddar and cream cheese in a food processor with the chopping blade inserted. Pulse to partially blend, then process until smooth, scraping down the sides of the work bowl often.

-Add the next 3 ingredients; process until well-blended. Put in a small bowl; cover and chill about 2 hours or until firm.

-Using the plastic wrap that you used to cover the cheese, shape the cheese into a firm ball. Place the nuts in a small bowl; roll the cheese ball to coat completely with nuts.

-It helps to quickly get a light coating all over the ball so that you can handle it easier to press it more firmly into the nuts to coat well. Once you have a good coating of nuts on it, you can reshape the ball if needed.

-Wrap in plastic wrap and keep chilled until serving time. Serve with low carb crackers and raw vegetables.

Makes 12 Balls

Per Serving: 88 Calories; 8g Fat; 3g Protein; 1g Carbohydrate; trace Dietary Fiber; .5g Net Carbs

SOUPS

Mushroom Crab Soup

Ingredients:

16 ounces fresh mushrooms, sliced

1 1/4 ounces onion, chopped, 1/4 cup

4 tablespoons butter

4 cups chicken broth

1/4 cup dry white wine

6 ounces crab meat

1/2 cup heavy cream

2 tablespoons fresh parsley, chopped

Salt and pepper, to taste

Directions:

-In a large pot, sauté the mushrooms and onion in butter until tender. Remove about half of the mushrooms and set aside.

-Add the broth and wine to the pot; puree soup in blender or with stick blender.

-Bring to a simmer, then stir in the crab meat, the reserved sliced mushrooms, cream and parsley; heat through. Season to taste.

Chunky Chicken Noodle Soup

Ingredients:

1 tablespoon oil

1 tablespoon butter

2 boneless chicken breasts, diced, 10-12 ounces

1/2 cup green pepper, chopped, 2 ounces

1/2 cup celery, sliced thin, 2 small stalks

1/2 cup fresh mushrooms, sliced, 2 ounces or 4 medium

1/4 cup onion, chopped, 1 1/4 ounces

2 cans chicken broth or 4 cups homemade broth

1 teaspoon chicken bouillon granules

1/2 cup water

1/2 cup carrots, sliced, 2 1/2 ounces or 1 medium carrot *

1 tablespoon fresh parsley, chopped

1/4 teaspoon pepper

Salt, to taste

Egg Noodles

Directions:

-Heat the oil and butter in a large saucepan over medium heat. Add the chicken; cook and stir 4-5 minutes or just until no longer pink. Add the green pepper, celery, mushrooms and onions. Cook and stir 7 minutes or until the vegetables are tender crisp.

-Add the broth, bouillon, water, carrots, parsley, pepper and salt. Simmer, uncovered, 15-20 minutes or until the carrots are tender. Add the Egg Noodles and simmer a few minutes until heated through.

Creamy Tomato Soup

Ingredients:

2 tablespoons butter

1/2 cup onion, 2 3/4 ounces

28 ounce can diced tomatoes, undrained

2 cups chicken broth, homemade preferred

1 cup heavy cream

Salt and pepper, to taste

2 tablespoons parsley, minced, optional

Directions:

-In a 3-quart pot, sauté the onion in butter until tender. Add the tomatoes, with their liquid, and broth; bring to a boil. Simmer 5 minutes.

-Puree with a stick blender until smooth. Stir in the cream and adjust the seasoning. Stir in the parsley and serve at once.

Creamy Southwestern Cheese Soup

Ingredients:

1 pound ground beef

2 3/4 ounces onion, chopped, 1/2 cup

2 cloves garlic, minced

1 tablespoon cumin

1 teaspoon chili powder

8 ounces cream cheese, softened

2 10-ounce cans Ro-tel tomatoes, undrained (tomatoes with green chilies)

2 14.5-ounce cans beef broth

1/2 cup heavy cream

2 teaspoons salt, or to taste

Directions:

-In a large soup pot, brown the ground beef with the onion and garlic; drain. Add the spices and cook a couple minutes.

-Drop the cream cheese in bits into the meat. With the back of a big spoon, smash it into the meat until no bits of white remain.

-Stir in remaining ingredients and heat through.

Creamy Nacho Soup

Ingredients:

1 pound pork sausage

1 small onion, diced, 2 1/2 ounces

1 medium cauliflower, 20 ounces

4 cups chicken broth

8 ounces cream cheese, softened

10 ounce can Ro-tel tomatoes, undrained (diced tomatoes with green chiles)

2 teaspoons salt or to taste

1/2 teaspoon pepper

1/2 teaspoon paprika, optional

2 tablespoons cilantro, chopped, optional

Directions:

-In a large soup pot, cook the sausage and onion; drain the fat. Remove from the pot and set aside.

-Cut the cauliflower into florets; add to the soup pot along with the broth and Ro-tel tomatoes. Bring to a boil; cover and simmer 25 minutes until the cauliflower is very tender.

-Cut the cream cheese into small cubes and add to the soup. Puree the soup with a stick blender until smooth. Stir in the sausage; heat through over medium-low heat. Adjust the seasoning and add the cilantro, if using.

Cheese Burger Soup

Ingredients:

1.5 lb ground beef

3 cups beef broth

8 oz. tomato paste

1½ tomatoes, chopped

½ red bell pepper, chopped

3 celery sticks, chopped

½ cup onions, chopped

1½ teaspoons parsley

1 teaspoon Worcestershire sauce

1 teaspoon garlic powder

½ teaspoon salt

½ teaspoon pepper

½ cup of cheese

2 slices bacon, cooked and chopped (optional)

Directions:

-Brown ground beef in a large sauce pan. Halfway through, drain as much fat as you can. Continue to cook meat while adding in onions, red pepper, and celery.

-Add cooked beef mixture and remaining ingredients to slow cooker. Stir to combine. Add more beef broth should you desire.

Creamy Asparagus Soup

Ingredients:

15 ounce can asparagus, reserve liquid

1 1/2 cups chicken broth, about

1/4 teaspoon marjoram

1/2 teaspoon onion powder

1/4 teaspoon garlic powder

1/4 teaspoon pepper

1/4 cup heavy cream

1 tablespoon fresh parsley

Salt, to taste

Directions:

-Add broth to the liquid from the can of asparagus to make 2 cups. If whole, chop the asparagus roughly.

-Put the asparagus, liquid from the can and the broth in a medium pot. Puree with an immersion blender until smooth.

-Add the seasonings and bring to a boil; turn down the heat. Add the cream and parsley and just heat through.

-Add salt, if needed.

Makes 2 Servings

Per Serving: 157 Calories; 13g Fat; 7g Protein; 5g Carbohydrate; 2g Dietary Fiber; 3g Net Carbs

Veggie Beef Soup

Ingredients:

3 pounds beef, cubed

6 cups water (can use part beef broth)

8 ounce can tomato sauce

2 1/2 ounces onion

1 clove garlic, minced

1 tablespoon salt

Dash pepper

1/4 teaspoon chili powder

1 bay leaf

1 cup celery, coarsely chopped, about 4 ounces

1 very small cabbage, about 13 ounces, coarsely chopped

1 cup fresh or frozen green beans, about 2 1/2 ounces

Directions:

-In a large kettle, heat some oil; brown the beef in the hot oil. Add the remaining ingredients; bring to a boil.

-Turn down the heat and simmer on low for about 2 hours.

Per Serving: 455 Calories; 33g Fat; 32g Protein; 6g Carbohydrate; 2g Dietary Fiber; 4g Net Carbs

Creamy Tuscan Soup

Ingredients:

1 pound Italian sausage

1 small onion, diced, 2 1/2 ounces

2 cloves garlic, minced

3 cups chicken broth

10 ounce package frozen chopped spinach, thawed

1/2 cup heavy cream

Salt and pepper, to taste

Freshly grated parmesan cheese, optional

Directions:

-Remove the sausage from its casings, if necessary. Brown the sausage in a 4-quart soup pot along with the onion and garlic; drain fat.

-Add the broth and undrained spinach; bring to a boil. Cover and simmer 30 minutes. Add the cream and simmer a few minutes until the cream is heated. Season to taste.

-Sprinkle a little parmesan cheese over each serving, if desired.

Makes 6 Servings

Per Serving: 366 Calories; 32g Fat; 15g Protein; 4g Carbohydrate; 2g Dietary Fiber; 2g Net Carbs

Seafood Bisque

Ingredients:

Small fresh cauliflower, about 1 pound

Small onion or leeks, minced, 2 1/2 ounces

3 cups chicken broth, homemade preferred

1/8 teaspoon Old Bay seasoning

1/8 teaspoon paprika

Salt and pepper, to taste

3 tablespoon butter

1/2 cup heavy cream

6 ounce can crab meat, drained

2 ounces tiny shrimp

Pinch fresh parsley

Pinch chives

Directions:

-Cut the cauliflower into small chunks. In a 4-quart pot or Dutch oven, place the cauliflower, onion and broth; season with salt and pepper.

-Bring to a boil; reduce heat and simmer, covered, about 25 minutes until very tender. Puree with a stick blender until thick and smooth.

-Add remaining ingredients; season to taste with salt and pepper. Reheat if necessary.

Makes 6 Servings

Per Serving: *200 Calories; 14g Fat; 12g Protein; 5g Carbohydrate; 2g Dietary Fiber; 3g Net Carbs*

Creamy Cauliflower Soup

Ingredients:

2 ounces onions, chopped, about 1/3 cup

1 tablespoon butter

2 cups chicken broth

2 cups water, optional

10 ounces frozen cauliflower or broccoli

Salt and pepper, to taste

1/2 cup heavy cream

Pinch parsley

Directions:

-In a medium to large pot, sauté the onions in the butter until soft. Add the broth and water, if using; bring to a boil.

-Stir in the frozen cauliflower; bring to a boil. Cover and simmer about 10 minutes until very tender.

-Puree with a stick blender, if desired, or just break up the cauliflower into tiny pieces. Stir in the cream and parsley.

Makes 3 Servings

Per Serving: 225 Calories; 20g Fat; 6g Protein; 7g Carbohydrate; 2g Dietary Fiber; 5g Net Carbs

BREAKFAST

Low Carb Cheesy Sausage and Egg Bake

Ingredients:

1 pound bulk pork sausage, cooked and drained

1 1/2 cups sliced fresh mushrooms (4 ounces)

8 medium green onions, sliced (1/2 cup)

2 medium tomatoes, seeded, chopped (1 1/2 cups)

2 cups shredded mozzarella cheese (8 ounces)

1 1/4 cups Original Bisquick™ mix

1 cup milk

1 1/2 teaspoons salt

1 1/2 teaspoons chopped fresh or 1/2 teaspoon dried oregano leaves

1/2 teaspoon pepper

12 eggs

Directions:

-Heat oven to 350°F. Grease rectangular baking dish, 13x9x2 inches. Layer sausage, mushrooms, onions, tomatoes and cheese in dish.

-Stir remaining ingredients until blended. Pour over cheese.

-Bake uncovered 30 to 35 minutes or until golden brown and set.

Ham Muffins

Ingredients:

12 ounces ham

1/4 cup green pepper, minced, 1 1/2 ounces

1 stalk celery, minced

1/4 teaspoon onion powder

1/4 teaspoon pepper

1 tablespoon chives, minced

1 tablespoon fresh parsley, chopped

Dash cayenne

3 eggs

6 ounces cheddar cheese, shredded

Directions:

-Grind the ham in a food processor until finely minced. Blend all of the ingredients in a large bowl. Spoon into 12 well-greased muffin cups.

-Place the muffin tin on a foil-lined rimmed baking sheet just in case the grease overflows.

-Bake at 350º 30-35 minutes until golden brown. Leave the muffins in the tin on a cooling rack for 10 minutes to allow them to set up a bit. Remove from the tin and serve hot with your choice of sauce.

Makes 12 Muffins

Per Serving: 129 Calories; 9g Fat; 10g Protein; 2g Carbohydrate; trace Dietary Fiber; 1.5g Net Carbs

Low Carb Good Morning Breakfast

Ingredients

12-16 ounces bacon, chopped and fried until crisp

1 pound pork sausage

1/2 cup onion, chopped, 2 1/2 ounces

1/2 cup green pepper, chopped, 1/2 medium

Other cooked meats of your choice, such as ham, roast beef, etc.

12 eggs

1 cup heavy cream

4 ounce can mushrooms, drained, optional

Salt and pepper, to taste

8 ounces cheddar cheese, shredded

Directions

-Brown the bacon, sausage, onions and peppers; drain the grease.

-Beat the eggs in a large bowl; beat in the cream.

-Add salt and pepper to taste. Arrange the meats, onion, green pepper, mushrooms and the cheese in a greased 9x13" baking dish. Pour the egg mixture evenly over everything.

-Cover and chill overnight, if desired. Bake at 350º for 50-60 minutes, until golden brown and a knife inserted comes out clean.

-If not chilled, bake about 40-45 minutes.

Makes 8 Servings

Per 1/8 Recipe: 846 Calories; 71g Fat; 46g Protein; 5g Carbohydrate; 1g Dietary Fiber; 4g Net Carbs

Low Carb Breakfast Balls

Ingredients:

1 lb turkey breakfast sausage, ground

1 lb extra lean ground beef (96% lean)

2 large eggs

2 tablespoons dried onion flakes

1/2 tsp black pepper

1/2 lb (8 oz) sharp cheddar cheese, shredded

Directions:

-Mix all the ingredients together until thoroughly blended (it is best to use an electric mixer).

-Form into about 5 dozen 1 inch balls and place on a cookie sheet or broiler pan.

-Bake at 375°F for about 25 minutes.

Makes 16 Balls

Broccoli Quiche with Ham

Ingredients:

6 eggs

3/4 cup heavy cream

1 teaspoon Dijon mustard

2 ounces onion, chopped, about 1/4 cup

10 ounce package frozen broccoli florets

8 ounce Swiss cheese, shredded

1/2 teaspoon salt

Dash pepper

2 cups ham, diced, about an 8 ounce package of sliced ham

Directions:

-Cook the broccoli and onion together until broccoli is tender. Drain very well.

-Grease a large pie plate; add the cheese, ham and broccoli and mix. Beat the eggs, cream, mustard, salt and pepper well with a whisk.

-Pour evenly over the broccoli mixture. Bake at 350º 35-45 minutes until a knife inserted in center comes out clean. Let stand 10 minutes before cutting.

Makes 6 Servings

Per 1/6 Recipe: 404 Calories; 31g Fat; 26g Protein; 2g Dietary Fiber; 5g Net Carbs

Onion & Bacon Pie

Ingredients:

5 slices bacon, chopped

1 large onion, sliced thin, 5 1/2 ounces

8 ounces Monterey jack cheese, shredded

6 eggs

1 cup heavy cream

1/2 teaspoon salt

1 teaspoon chili powder

Directions:

-Sauté the bacon and onion until the bacon is cooked and the onion is tender and slightly caramelized. Place the cheese in a greased pie plate; top with the bacon and onions.

-Beat the eggs, cream and seasonings; pour over everything. Bake at 350º for 35-40 minutes until a knife inserted in the center comes out clean.

-Let stand 10 minutes before cutting.

Makes 6 Servings

Per 1/6 Recipe: 393 Calories; 34g Fat; 18g Protein; 4g Carbohydrate; 1g Dietary Fiber; 3g Net Carbs

Bacon Cheese Frittata

Ingredients:

6 eggs

1 cup heavy cream

1/2 teaspoon salt

1/4 teaspoon pepper

2 green onions, chopped

5 slices bacon, fried until crisp

4 ounces cheddar cheese

Directions:

-Beat the eggs, cream and seasonings.

-Pour into a large greased pie plate. Top with the remaining ingredients and bake at 350º 30-35 minutes. Let stand a few minutes before serving.

Makes 6 Servings

Per Serving: 320 Calories; 29g Fat; 13g Protein; 2g Carbohydrate; trace Dietary Fiber; 2g Net Carbs

Low Carb Breakfast Skillet

Ingredients:

6 large eggs

1/2 package of bacon

2 tbsp of salted Butter

2 tsp of pepper

1/2 medium onion

1 cup cheddar cheese

Directions:

-Cook bacon, while the bacon is cooking, dice up the 1/2 onion. Place the pepper, butter, and onions into a skillet over medium heat and cook until the onions are lightly brown, stirring occasionally.

-Scramble the eggs in a mixing bowl while waiting for your onions to brown. Once the onions are lightly brown, pour in the eggs and cook until eggs are done.'

-Add the cheese to the eggs, and mix until the cheese is melted.

-Crumble up the crisp bacon, and add it to the mix. Serve in a bowl

Makes 2 Servings

Per Serving: Calories 751.7, Total Fat: 61.0 g, Cholesterol: 754.3 mg, Sodium: 1,130.1 mg,Total Carbs: 6.5 g, Dietary Fiber: 1.1 g, Protein: 43.1 g

Low Carb Chicken Fajita Omelet

Ingredients:

1 tablespoon butter

2 eggs, beaten

2 ounces leftover sliced fajita chicken, about 1/2 cup

2 tablespoons leftover sautéed peppers and onions

1/2 ounce cheddar cheese, shredded

2 tablespoons salsa

1 tablespoon sour cream

Directions:

-Heat the butter in a large nonstick skillet over medium heat. When the butter is hot, pour in the beaten eggs; tilt the pan to spread the egg to cover bottom of the pan evenly.

-Lightly sprinkle with salt and pepper; let cook until the egg starts to set and, but is still moist. Arrange the chicken slices down the center of the omelet and top with the pepper and onion mixture.

-Sprinkle the cheese over the peppers. Let cook until the egg looks set, but not dry. With a spatula, fold the sides of the omelet over the filling in center.

-Let cook a few seconds to melt the cheese. Slide the omelet onto a serving plate. Top with salsa and sour cream.

Makes 1 Serving

Per serving: 394 Calories; 31g Fat; 23g Protein; 7g Carbohydrate; 1g Dietary Fiber; 6g Net Carbs

ENTREES

Creamed Chicken

Ingredients:

1/4 cup butter

1 small onion, diced, 2 1/2 ounces

2 stalks celery, diced, 4 ounces

1 small carrot, diced, 2 ounces

1/2 cup plus 1 tablespoon Carbalose flour

2 cups chicken broth

1 cup heavy cream

2 cups diced, cooked chicken

Salt and pepper, to taste

3 tablespoons fresh parsley, chopped

1/4 cup frozen peas, optional

Directions:

-In a large pot, sauté the onion, celery and carrots in the butter until very tender, about 10 minutes. Stir in the flour and mix until no dry flour remains.

-Stir in the broth and the cream; bring to a boil, stirring constantly until thickened. Add the chicken, seasonings, parsley and peas, if using.

-Heat just until the peas are hot; don't overcook them. Serve over hot biscuits

Makes 6 Servings

Per Serving: 351 Calories; 27g Fat; 20g Protein; 9g Carbohydrate; 4g Dietary Fiber; 5g Net Carbs

Zucchini Pasta with Sausage

Ingredients:

1 batch Sicilian-Style Hot Turkey Sausage

1 clove garlic, minced

14.5 ounce can diced tomatoes, drained

1 teaspoon Italian seasoning

2 medium zucchini, julienned, about 1 1/4 pound before trimming

Salt and pepper, to taste

Pinch fresh basil, optional

1/2 cup freshly grated parmesan cheese, 2 ounces

Directions:

-In a large skillet, brown the sausage with the garlic; drain off any excess grease. Add the tomatoes and Italian seasoning.

-Simmer, uncovered, for a few minutes. Add the zucchini and cook just until it is tender but not mushy.

-Adjust the seasoning with salt and pepper. Sprinkle with the basil and parmesan cheese to serve.

Makes 4 Servings

Per Serving: 369 Calories; 25g Fat; 28g Protein; 8g Carbohydrate; 2g Dietary Fiber; 6g Net Carbs

Chicken with Peanut Curry Sauce

Ingredients:

2 tablespoons oil

1 1/2 pounds boneless chicken breast, cubed

Salt and pepper, to taste

8 ounces frozen cut green beans, thawed

8 ounces frozen bell pepper strips, thawed

Sauce:

13.5 ounces coconut milk (1 can)

1/2 cup chicken broth

1 tablespoon red Thai curry paste

1/3 cup natural peanut butter

2 tablespoon granular Splenda or equivalent liquid Splenda

1 tablespoon lime juice

Cilantro for garnish, optional

Directions:

-In a 4-cup measuring cup, whisk together all of the sauce ingredients except the cilantro; set aside.

-Heat the oil in a large skillet over medium-high heat. Sauté the chicken just until the outside is opaque. Add the green beans and peppers; cook another 3 minutes, stirring frequently.

-Add the sauce to the skillet with the chicken and vegetables. Bring to a boil then turn down the heat and simmer 6-8 minutes until the sauce thickens slightly. Sprinkle with cilantro to serve.

Makes 4-6 servings

Per 1/4 Recipe: 608 Calories; 38g Fat; 48g Protein; 16g Carbohydrate; 4g Dietary Fiber; 12g Net Carbs

Skillet Chicken Florentine

Ingredients:

2 tablespoons butter, divided

3 boneless chicken breasts or 6 chicken tenders (about 1 pound)

10 ounces frozen chopped spinach, thawed

2 cloves garlic, minced

1/4 cup heavy cream

1/4 cup parmesan cheese

Salt and pepper, to taste

Directions:

-Season the chicken with salt and pepper. Heat 1 tablespoon butter in a large skillet over medium-high heat.

-Brown the chicken about 1 1/2 to 2 minutes per side, but do not cook all the way through. Remove the chicken to a plate.

-Add the other tablespoon of butter to the skillet and heat over medium-low heat. Add the spinach and garlic; cook about 1 minute, just to heat.

-Stir in the cream and cheese. Adjust the seasonings with salt and pepper, as needed, then spread the spinach evenly over the bottom of the skillet.

-Top the spinach with the chicken in a single layer; cover the pan and simmer over low heat about 5 minutes or so or just until the chicken is done to your liking. Serve the chicken topped with the spinach mixture.

Makes 3 Servings

Per Serving: 334 Calories; 20g Fat; 33g Protein; 5g Carbohydrate; 3g Dietary Fiber; 2g Net Carbs

Taco Skillet

Ingredients:

2 pounds ground beef

1 medium onion, chopped, 4 ounces

2 cloves garlic, minced

3 tablespoons Seasoning for Tacos

14.5 ounce can diced tomatoes, undrained

16 ounces coleslaw mix or shredded cabbage

Salt, to taste

4 ounces sharp cheddar cheese, shredded

6 tablespoons sour cream, optional

Cilantro, optional

Directions:

-Brown the meat with the onion and garlic in a large skillet; drain the grease. Add the seasoning and tomatoes. Simmer, uncovered, 5 minutes.

-Add the cabbage and cook, uncovered, 5 minutes, stirring occasionally. Add salt to taste, if needed. Sprinkle the cheese over the top, cover and cook 2 minutes until the cheese melts.

-Stir in the cheese. Top each serving with 1 tablespoon sour cream and a pinch of cilantro, if you like, but they are not included in the counts.

Makes 6 Servings

Per Serving: 383 Calories; 24g Fat; 32g Protein; 11g Carbohydrate; 3g Dietary Fiber; 8g Net Carbs

Cabbage Roll Skillet

Ingredients:

2 pounds ground beef

1 medium onion (6 ounces before trimming)

1 clove garlic, minced

1 small-medium cabbage, chopped (2 pounds cabbage before trimming)

28 ounce can crushed tomatoes

1 teaspoon salt, or to taste

1 teaspoon pepper, or to taste

2 tablespoons vinegar

2 tablespoons granular Splenda or equivalent liquid Splenda

Directions:

-In a very large skillet, wok or Dutch oven, brown the ground beef with the onion and garlic; drain the fat, if desired.

-Stir in the remaining ingredients. Cover and simmer 30-40 minutes or until the cabbage is tender.

Makes 6 Servings

Per 1/6 Recipe: 338 Calories; 18g Fat; 28g Protein; 6g Dietary Fiber; 12g Net Carbs

Spicy Beef And Pepper Skillet Dinner

Ingredients:

2 pounds ground beef

1 small onion, sliced thin, 2 1/2 ounces

1 teaspoon ginger, grated

1/4 teaspoon xanthan gum, optional

1 green pepper, cut into strips, about 4 ounces

1 red pepper, cut into strips, about 4 ounces

Sauce:

1/4 cup soy sauce

1/2 teaspoon crushed red pepper

1 teaspoon granular Splenda

1/4 teaspoon salt

1/2 teaspoon pepper

1 tablespoon sesame oil

Salt, to taste

Directions:

-Mix the sauce ingredients in a small bowl. In a large skillet or wok, brown the meat with the onion and ginger; drain the grease.

-Add the peppers and cook until tender-crisp. Sprinkle the xanthan gum over the meat and quickly mix in well. Pour in the sauce mixture and bring to a boil; simmer until the sauce has thickened.

-Adjust the seasoning, if necessary.

Makes 6 Servings

Per Serving: 296 Calories; 19g Fat; 25g Protein; 4g Carbohydrate; 1g Dietary Fiber; 3g Net Carbs

Cheesy Pork Casserole

Ingredients:

16 ounce bag frozen cauliflower

Salt and pepper, to taste

3 ounces cream cheese with chives and onions

2 tablespoons heavy cream

8 ounces cheddar cheese, shredded

4 servings leftover roast pork, cubed

Directions:

-Cook the cauliflower until very tender; drain. Put the cauliflower in a 1 1/2 quart casserole; season well with salt and pepper.

-In a 4-cup glass measure, heat the cream cheese, cream and cheddar cheese (reserve a little cheese for top, if desired) in the microwave on MEDIUM for about 2-3 minutes, stirring occasionally until creamy.

-Pour the cheese mixture over the cauliflower and mix well. Stir in the cubed pork; season to taste. Top with the reserved cheese. Bake at 350° for 35 minutes, until bubbly and starting to brown on top.

Makes 4 Servings

Per Serving: 484 Calories; 38g Fat; 30g Protein; 8g Carbohydrate; 3g Dietary Fiber; 5g Net Carbs

Creamy Mushroom Chicken Casserole

Ingredients:

3-4 cups diced cooked chicken

1 pound pork sausage

1 stalk celery, chopped fine

1 tablespoon onion, chopped

1/2 pound mushrooms, sliced

8 ounces cream cheese, softened

16 ounce bag frozen cauliflower, cooked well and drained

8 ounces cheddar cheese, shredded

Salt

1/2 teaspoon pepper

Paprika, optional

Directions:

-Brown the sausage with the celery, onion and mushrooms. Stir the softened cream cheese into the sausage mixture until well blended.

-Coarsely chop the cooked cauliflower. Mix all of the ingredients and spread in a greased 9x13" baking dish. If desired, dust the top with paprika.

-Bake at 350º for about 40 minutes until the top is nicely browned.

Makes 8 Servings

Per 1/8 Recipe: 550 Calories; 40g Fat; 42g Protein; 6g Carbohydrate; 2g Dietary Fiber; 4g Net Carbs

Spinach and Sausage Casserole

Ingredients:

1 pound bulk pork sausage

10 ounce package frozen chopped spinach, thawed and well-drained

8 ounce cream cheese, softened

1/3 cup sour cream

4 ounces cheddar cheese, shredded

2 teaspoons Seasoning for Tacos

10 ounce can Ro-tel tomatoes, drained (diced tomatoes with green chiles)

1/4 cup canned sliced pickled jalapeños

Directions:

-Brown the sausage; drain the fat. Put in a greased 2 1/2-quart casserole along with all of the remaining ingredients.

-Mix well and bake at 350° for about 40 minutes or until bubbly and browned on top.

Makes 6 Servings

Per 1/6 Recipe: 503 Calories; 43g Fat; 25g Protein; 7g Carbohydrate; 2g Dietary Fiber; 5g Net Carbs

Swiss Mushroom Chicken

Ingredients:

4 boneless chicken breasts, pounded flat if desired

Salt, pepper and your choice of seasonings

1/2 pound mushrooms, sliced

2 tablespoons butter

4 thin slices deli ham

4 slices Swiss cheese, about 1 ounce each

Directions:

-Season the chicken as desired; grill or sauté till just done. Place the chicken in a large baking dish.

-Sauté the mushrooms in the butter until tender. Top each piece of chicken with a slice of ham, 1/4 of the mushrooms, then a slice of cheese.

-Bake at 350º for 15-20 minutes until everything is hot and the cheese is melted.

-Makes 4 Servings

Per Serving: 325 Calories; 15g Fat; 41g Protein; 3g Carbohydrate; 1g Dietary Fiber; 2g Net Carbs

Italian Chicken

Ingredients:

8 chicken thighs, skin removed

8 ounces tomato sauce

2 tablespoons tomato paste

1/4 teaspoon onion powder

1/4 teaspoon garlic powder

1/4 teaspoon Italian seasoning

1/4 teaspoon salt, or to taste

4 ounce can mushrooms, drained

8 ounces mozzarella cheese, shredded

1/4 cup parmesan cheese, 1 ounce

Directions:

-Place the chicken in a greased 9x13" glass baking dish. Mix all the remaining ingredients except the cheeses.

-Spoon the sauce over the chicken. Cover with plastic wrap and microwave on MEDIUM power 30 minutes until the chicken is cooked through.

-Top with the cheeses and cook, uncovered, on MEDIUM 5 minutes until the cheese is melted and bubbly. Let stand 5 minutes before serving.

Makes 4-8 servings

Per Thigh: 198 Calories; 10g Fat; 21g Protein; 4g Carbohydrate; 1g Dietary Fiber; 3g Net Carbs

Sweet And Sour Chicken

Ingredients:

3 boneless chicken breasts

Salt, pepper and garlic powder

1 tablespoon oil

2 green peppers, coarsely chopped

1 small onion, coarsely chopped, 2 1/2 ounces

1 medium carrot, sliced on the bias, 2 ounces

1 clove garlic, minced

SAUCE:

1/2 cup cider vinegar

1/2 cup chicken broth

1 teaspoon blackstrap molasses

2/3 cup granular Splenda or equivalent liquid Splenda

1/2 teaspoon ground ginger or a pinch of freshly grated ginger

2 tablespoons low carb Ketchup

2 tablespoon soy sauce

2 tablespoon rice wine or dry white wine

2 tablespoon sugar free syrup, pineapple flavor

1/2 teaspoon xanthan gum

Directions:

-To prepare the sauce, mix all of the ingredients together except the xanthan gum in a small saucepan. Bring to a boil.

-Lightly sprinkle the xanthan gum a little at a time over the surface and briskly whisk in until the sauce thickens; set aside. You can make the sauce up to several days ahead of time and store in the refrigerator.

-Season the chicken with salt, pepper and garlic powder. Grill or pan fry the chicken until just barely done; cut into bite-size pieces and set aside.

-Heat the oil in a wok or large nonstick skillet over medium-high heat. Stir-fry the peppers, onion, carrot and garlic until the peppers and carrot are almost crisp-tender.

-Add the sauce to the wok; cook until bubbly. Stir in the chicken and cook until heated through. Serve over chopped iceberg lettuce, if desired.

Makes 5 Servings

Per Serving: 146 Calories; 4g Fat; 18g Protein; 9g Carbohydrate; 2g Dietary Fiber; 7g Net Carbs

Chicken Breasts with Garlic & Parsley

Ingredients:

3 boneless chicken breasts, cubed

2 tablespoons Carbalose flour

1/2 teaspoon salt

1/2 teaspoon pepper

2 tablespoons oil

1 tablespoon garlic, minced

3 tablespoons fresh parsley, chopped

2 tablespoons butter

Directions:

-Pat the chicken dry with paper towels and toss with the flour, salt and pepper. Heat the oil in a large skillet over high heat. Cook the chicken 3 1/2 minutes, turning occasionally.

-Add the garlic, parsley and butter. Sauté 1 minute and stir to coat the chicken with the pan sauce.

Makes 4 Servings

Per Serving: 223 Calories; 14g Fat; 22g Protein; 3g Carbohydrate; 1.5g Dietary Fiber; 1.5g Net Carbs

Broccoli and Chicken Stir-Fry

Ingredients:

1 pound boneless chicken thighs, cut in bite-size pieces

1 tablespoon oil

12 ounces fresh broccoli florets

4 cloves garlic, minced

4 green onions, sliced

1-2 teaspoons ground ginger

1/2 teaspoon xanthan gum (optional)

Sauce:

1/4 cup soy sauce

2 tablespoons rice vinegar

2 packets True Orange or other orange flavoring equal to about 2 tablespoons orange juice

2 tablespoons granular Splenda or equivalent liquid sweetener

1/2 teaspoon sesame oil

1 teaspoon chili paste (sambal oelek)

Directions:

-Heat the oil in a large skillet or wok over medium-high heat. Add the chicken; cook until the chicken is done, stirring occasionally, about 6 minutes.

-Meanwhile, mix the sauce ingredients in a small bowl and microwave the broccoli florets, in a covered casserole or the bag it came in, for 2 minutes on HIGH.

-Mix the ginger and xanthan gum in a small bowl.

Makes 3 Servings

Per Serving: 193 Calories; 10g Fat; 15g Protein; 14g Carbohydrate; 5g Dietary Fiber; 9g Net Carbs

Low Carb Cajun Chicken

Ingredients:

3 boneless chicken breasts, sliced in thin strips

2 teaspoons Cajun Seasoning

3 tablespoons butter

1 tablespoon oil

3 medium green and/or red bell peppers, cut in thin strips, 8 ounces

1/2 pound mushrooms, sliced

4 green onions, cut diagonally in 1/2-inch pieces

1/8 teaspoon basil

1/8 teaspoon garlic powder

1/8 teaspoon pepper

1/4 teaspoon salt, or to taste

1/4 cup heavy cream

1/2 teaspoon xanthan gum

Directions:

-In a medium bowl, toss the chicken pieces with the Cajun seasoning. Heat the butter and oil in a large, nonstick skillet or wok on medium-high heat.

-Stir-fry the chicken until it's not quite done. Don't overcook it as it will get further cooking with the remaining ingredients. Add the peppers and mushrooms. Stir-fry until the peppers are crisp-tender.

-If using xanthan gum, mix with seasonings in a small bowl. Reduce heat to low and stir in seasonings and then the cream. Cook just until sauce thickens. Add green onions and toss briefly to combine.

-Season with more salt, if needed; serve at once.

Makes 4 Servings

Per Serving: 287 Calories; 19g Fat; 22g Protein; 7g Carbohydrate; 3g Dietary Fiber; 4g Net Carbs

Low Carb Grilled Teriyaki Chicken

Ingredients:

1/3 cup water

1/4 cup dry sherry

1/4 cup soy sauce

2 cloves garlic, minced

1/4-1/2 teaspoon ground ginger

3 boneless chicken breasts

Directions:

-Mix all but the chicken in a 2 cup measuring cup. Place the chicken in a large zipper bag and add the marinade mixture.

-Place the bag in a shallow pan and marinate in the refrigerator at least 2 hours, turning the bag over occasionally. Drain and discard the marinade. Grill the chicken on indoor or outdoor grill just until the chicken is no longer pink in the center.

-Be careful not to overcook it.

Makes 3 Servings

Per Serving: 140 Calories; 1g Fat; 28g Protein; 1g Carbohydrate; trace Dietary Fiber; 1g Net Carbs

Chicken Parmesan

Ingredients:

1 boneless chicken breast, pounded thin

1 egg, beaten

Parmesan cheese, enough to coat the chicken

Dash garlic powder

Salt and pepper, to taste

1 tablespoon spaghetti sauce

1 ounce mozzarella cheese, shredded

Directions:

-Dip the chicken in egg, then coat with parmesan cheese. Sauté in oil until browned on both sides; season with garlic powder, salt and pepper.

-Place in a baking dish and spread with sauce. Top with the mozzarella. Microwave on MEDIUM for about 5 minutes until cheese is melted.

Makes 1 Serving

Per Serving: 387 Calories; 19g Fat; 48g Protein; 3g Carbohydrate; trace Dietary Fiber; 3g Net Carbs

Low Carb Mushroom Chicken Dinner

Ingredients:

6 chicken thighs

Salt

1/8 teaspoon pepper

1/4 teaspoon paprika

Sauce:

1/4 cup butter

1/2 pound mushrooms, sliced

1 teaspoon soy sauce

1/2 teaspoon Dijon mustard

3/4 cup heavy cream

Dash paprika

Pinch fresh parsley, chopped

Salt and pepper, to taste

Directions:

-Season the chicken and place in a large baking pan. Bake at 425º for 45 minutes, until done. About 20 minutes before chicken is done, melt the butter in a large skillet.

-Sauté the mushrooms until tender. Stir in the soy sauce and mustard, then slowly stir in the cream. Bring to a boil and cook until the sauce has thickened. Season to taste and stir in parsley.

-Serve over the chicken.

Makes 6 Servings

Per Serving: 378 Calories; 33g Fat; 17g Protein; 2g Carbohydrate; 1g Dietary Fiber; 1g Net Carbs

SLOW COOKER

Hot Wing Dip

Ingredients

8 ounces reduced-fat cream cheese (Neufchatel), cut up

1/4-1/2 cup bottled Buffalo wing sauce

1 1/2 tablespoons bottled reduced-calorie blue cheese salad dressing

1 cup chopped cooked chicken breast

1 stalk celery, finely chopped (1/2 cup)

1 fresh jalapeno chile pepper, seeded and minced*

20 stalks celery, halved crosswise

Directions

In a 1 1/2-quart slow cooker combine cream cheese, wing sauce, dressing, chicken, finely chopped celery, and jalapeno pepper.

Cover and cook on low-heat setting for 3 to 4 hours. If no heat setting is available, cook for 3 hours. Serve with celery pieces.

Number of Servings: 10

Total Carbs: 3g per serving

Broccoli Cheese Dip

Ingredients:

1 8 - ounce package reduced-fat cream cheese (Neufchatel), cut up

6 ounces reduced-fat pasteurized prepared cheese product

1 1/2 cups broccoli, blanched* and chopped

3 tablespoons bottled salsa

4 teaspoons bacon-flavor vegetable protein bits

Fat-free milk (optional)

1 recipe Potato Dippers

Directions:

In a 1 1/2- or 2-quart slow cooker combine cream cheese, cheese product, broccoli, salsa, and bacon-flavor bits.

Cover and cook on low-heat setting for 4 hours or on high-heat setting for 2 hours. If no heat setting is available, cook for 3 hours.

Stir dip before serving. If desired, thin dip to desired consistency with milk.

Number of Servings: 16

Total Carbs: 12g

Barbeque Turkey Wedges

Ingredients:

Nonstick cooking spray

1 pound lean ground turkey

3/4 cup finely chopped red onion

3 cloves garlic, minced

1 14 1/2 - ounce can no-salt-added diced tomatoes, undrained

1/3 cup bottled barbecue sauce

1/4 teaspoon black pepper

1/2 small cucumber, seeded and chopped (1/2 cup)

1 recipe Pita Wedges

Pita Wedges:

2 6 - inches whole wheat pita rounds

Directions:

Coat a large unheated skillet with cooking spray. Cook turkey, 1/2 cup of the onion, and the garlic in skillet over medium-high heat for 5 to 8 minutes or until turkey is brown and onion is tender, stirring frequently. Drain fat.

Stir in tomatoes, barbecue sauce, and pepper; heat through. Transfer mixture to a 1 1/2- or 2-quart slow cooker. Cover and keep warm on the keep-warm setting for up to 2 hours.

Just before serving, sprinkle turkey mixture in cooker with remaining chopped onion and cucumber. Serve turkey mixture with Pita Wedges.

Pita Wedges:

Preheat oven to 350 degrees F. Split pita bread rounds in half horizontally. Cut each half into eight wedges. Arrange wedges in a single layer on a baking sheet. Bake for 10 to 15 minutes or until lightly browned and crisp; let cool.

Number of Servings: 16

Total Carbs: 8g per serving

Italian Cocktail Meatballs:

Ingredients:

1 12 - ounce package refrigerated or frozen cooked turkey meatballs, thawed (12)

1/2 cup bottled roasted red and/or yellow sweet peppers, drained and cut into 1-inch pieces

1/8 teaspoon crushed red pepper

1 cup bottled reduced-sodium pasta sauce

Snipped fresh basil (optional)

Directions:

In a 1 1/2- or 2-quart slow cooker combine meatballs and roasted peppers. Sprinkle with crushed red pepper. Pour pasta sauce over all in cooker.

Cover and cook on low-heat setting for 4 to 5 hours or on high-heat setting for 2 to 2 1/2 hours. If no heat setting is available, cook for 4 to 5 hours.

Skim fat from sauce. Stir meatballs gently before serving. Serve immediately or keep warm, covered, on warm- or low-heat setting (if available) for up to 2 hours. If desired, garnish with basil.

Number of Servings: 12

Total Carbs: 3g per serving

Fruit Chutney with Spiced Chips

Ingredients:

2 large apples, cored and cut into 1-inch pieces

2 large pears, cored and cut into 1-inch pieces

1 sweet onion, chopped

1 cup fresh or frozen whole cranberries, thawed

1/3 cup packed brown sugar*

1/4 cup balsamic vinegar

1 teaspoon ground cinnamon

1 teaspoon ground ginger

1/8 teaspoon salt

1 tablespoon cornstarch

2 tablespoons cold water

1 recipe Spiced Chips

4 ounces goat cheese , crumbled

Directions

For fruit chutney, in a 3 1/2- or 4-quart slow cooker combine apples, pears, onion, cranberries. brown sugar, vinegar, cinnamon, ginger, and salt.

Cover and cook on high-heat setting for 1 hour. In a small bowl combine cornstarch and the cold water; stir into cooker. Cover and cook on high-heat setting for 1 hour more.

Serve chutney warm or at room temperature with Spiced Chips and top each serving with crumbled goat cheese.

Number of Servings: 24

Total Carbs: 21g

:

5 Spice Chicken Wings

Ingredients:

16 chicken wings (about 3 pounds)

3/4 cup bottled plum sauce

1 tablespoon butter, melted

1 teaspoon five-spice powder

Slivered green onions (optional)

Directions:

Preheat oven to 375 degrees F. Using a sharp knife, carefully cut off tips of the wings; discard wing tips. Cut each wing at joint to make two pieces.

In a foil-lined 15x10x1-inch baking pan arrange wing pieces in a single layer. Bake for 20 minutes. Drain well.

In a 3 1/2- or 4-quart slow cooker combine plum sauce, butter, and five-spice powder. Add chicken pieces, stirring to coat with sauce.

Cover and cook on low-heat setting for 3 to 4 hours or on high-heat setting for 1 1/2 to 2 hours.

Serve immediately or keep warm, covered, on warm- or low-heat setting for up to 1 hour. If desired, sprinkle with slivered green onions.

Number of Servings: 32

Total Carbs: 3g per serving

Thai Chicken Wings with Peanut Sauce

Ingredients:

24 chicken wing drummettes (about 2 1/4 pounds)

1/4 cup water

1 tablespoon lime juice

1/4 teaspoon ground ginger

1 recipe Peanut Sauce (below)

Peanut Sauce

1/2 cup creamy peanut butter

1/2 cup water

2 tablespoons reduced-sodium soy sauce

2 cloves garlic, minced

1/2 teaspoon ground ginger

1/4 teaspoon crushed red pepper

Directions:

Place chicken in a 3 1/2- or 4-quart slow cooker. Add the water, lime juice, and ginger to cooker.

Cover and cook on low-heat setting for 5 to 6 hours or on high-heat setting for 2 1/2 to 3 hours.

Prepare Peanut Sauce. Drain chicken, discarding cooking liquid. Toss chicken with half of the Peanut Sauce. If desired, return chicken to slow cooker. Serve immediately or keep warm, covered, on warm- or low-heat setting for up to 1 hour. Serve with remaining sauce (whisk sauce if it looks separated).

For Sauce:

In a small saucepan whisk together creamy peanut butter, water, soy sauce, garlic, ginger, and crushed red pepper. Heat over medium-low heat until mixture is smooth, whisking constantly. Makes about 1 cup.

Number of Servings:12

Total Carbs: 3g per serving

Bourbon Glazed Cocktail Sausages

Ingredients:

16 ounces light, cooked smoked Polish sausage or smoked turkey sausage, cut into 1-inch slices

⅓ cup low-sugar apricot preserves

3 tablespoons pure maple syrup

1 tablespoon bourbon or water

1 teaspoon quick-cooking tapioca, crushed

Directions:

In a 1- ½-quart slow cooker combine sausage slices, apricot preserves, maple syrup, bourbon, and tapioca. Cover and cook on low-heat setting for 4 hours. If no heat setting is available, cook for 4 hours.

Serve immediately or keep warm in the slow cooker for up to 1 hour. Serve with wooden toothpicks.

Tip: For easy cleanup, line your slow cooker with a disposable slow cooker liner. Add ingredients as directed in recipe. Once your dish is finished cooking, spoon the food out of your slow cooker and simply dispose of the liner. Do not lift or transport the disposable liner with food inside.

Total Carbs: 7g per serving (2)

Low Carb Pumpkin and Sausage Soup

Ingredients:

16 oz. country style sausage
1 small onion, minced
1 clove garlic, minced
1 tbsp italian seasoning
1 cup fresh mushrooms, chopped
1 can (15 oz.) pumpkin
5 cups chicken broth, reduced-sodium
1/2 cup heavy cream
1/2 cup sour cream
1/2 cup water

Directions:

-Over medium heat cook the sausage breaking into small bits. Drain fat.

-Add the onion, garlic, Italian seasoning, and mushrooms, and cook and stir until vegetables are tender.

-Add the canned pumpkin, and the broth, stirring to mix well.

-Cook at a low simmer for 20 to 30-minutes.

-Remove from heat and stir in heavy cream, sour cream and water. Serve warm. This soup freezes well in single-serving portions.

Number of Servings: 8

Total Carbs: 7.4

Low Carb Shrimp and Meatball Gumbo

Ingredients:

8 oz lean ground beef
1/2 lb raw 6/80 count shrimp, shelled
1 can of tomato sauce
1 small onion, chopped
1/2 green bell pepper, chopped
1 bag okra
2 qts chicken broth
basil, thyme, old bay, salt, pepper, to taste

Directions:

-Add the broth to a large pot and bring to a boil.

-Add the chopped veggies , the okra, the tomato sauce, and spices to taste.

-Bring to a boil, then reduce to a simmer. Add the ground beef made into meatball shapes (you can brown beforehand if desired).

-Simmer until the veggies are cooked, then add the shrimp and simmer for another 3-5 minutes.

Number of Servings: 4

Total Carbs: 9.5

Slow Cooker French Onion Soup

Ingredients:

4 sweet onions, sliced

2 tablespoons butter

1 tablespoon Worcestershire sauce

1 tablespoon balsamic vinegar

3 garlic cloves, minced

2 teaspoon brown sugar

1/2 teaspoon pepper

1/2 teaspoon salt

3 tablespoon all-purpose flour

64 oz vegetable broth (or chicken broth or beef broth)

2 tablespoon fresh thyme

Directions:

-Set your crockpot to high and add the onions, butter, Worcestershire sauce, vinegar, garlic, brown sugar, salt, and pepper. Cook for 60 minutes until onions begin to brown and caramelize, stirring occasionally.

-Stir in the flour and let cook for 5 more minutes.

-Add the broth and thyme. Cook on low for 6-8 hours.

-To serve with bread and cheese, slice a small piece of french bread and place on top of the soup. Cover with one slice of Swiss cheese and broil for 3 minutes.

Total Carbs: 20g

Low Carb Turkey Soup

Ingredients:

½ tablespoon extra light olive oil

½ cup onion - raw, chopped

1 cup diced celery (raw)

2 cups chopped turkey breast

2 cups of chopped dark turkey meat

2 cans of chicken broth

4 cups of turkey broth

1 cup of fresh mushrooms (sliced)

6 medium sized asparagus

2 cups of fresh shredded cabbage

1 cup of fresh spinach

1 cup water

Directions:

-Soften celery and onion in a skillet with 1/2 tablespoon olive oil. In the meantime, chop all your veggies to the desired size.

-Add all broth and water to crock pot.

-Next, add in chopped turkey meat and veggies. Salt and pepper to taste.

-Cook on low 4-6 hours or until veggies are soft

Number of Servings: 8

Total Carbs: 5.3g

Potato Soup

Ingredients:

6 large potatoes, cubed

3 large carrots, sliced

3 stalks celery, chopped

2 onions, chopped

4 chicken bouillon cubes

6 cups of water

1 can non-fat evaporated milk

shredded cheddar cheese (optional, to desired preferance)

Directions:

-Combine all vegetables, bouillon, and water in large crock pot.

-Cook on low for 8 - 10 hours, or high 3 -4.

-Add evaporated milk, stir till heated through, and serve.

(May serve with shredded cheddar cheese)

Number of Servings: 15

Chicken Tortilla Soup

Ingredients:

3 raw boneless, skinless chicken breasts

1 (15 ounce) can diced tomatoes

1 (10 ounce) can enchilada sauce

1 medium onion, chopped

1 (4 ounce) can chopped green chile peppers

3 cloves garlic, minced

2 cups water

1 (14.5 ounce) can 99% fat-free chicken broth

1 tablespoon cumin

1 tablespoon chili powder

1 teaspoon salt

1/4 teaspoon black pepper

1 bay leaf

1 (10 ounce) package frozen corn

1 tablespoon chopped cilantro

Directions:

-Combine all ingredients in a large slow cooker. Stir to combine. Cook on high 4-6 hours or low 6-8 hours.

-Remove chicken from soup and shred. Return chicken to soup, stir, and serve.

-If you like things spicy and flavorful, also add in a dash or two of cayenne.

Number of Servings: 8

Total Carbs: 11.7g

Low Carb Steak and Smoked Sausage Chili

Ingredients:

2lb - steak (can be any type you desire)

16oz - smoked sausage (again- your preference)

1 green pepper

1 red pepper

1 onion

1 tbsp of olive oil

3 petite diced tomatoes

2pg – 'McCormick' Chili seasoning

1 tbsp chili powder

1 tbsp garlic powder

1 tbsp cayenne pepper powder

Directions:

-Start cubing the steak to desired size.

-Throw it in a heated 5qt pot w/oil and brown, use garlic and chili powder (desired amount) to flavor steak.

-Slice smoked sausage and add to pot once the steak is browned.

-Dice green peppers, red peppers, and onion. Add the petite diced tomatoes, McCormick chili seasoning mix and if any remaining spices dump them in if you so choose.

-Only use desired amount of cayenne pepper for spice. Can be substituted or increased for level of spice.

Number of Servings: 16

Total Carbs: 8.2

Low Carb Salsa Chicken

Ingredients:

4 boneless, skinless chicken breast

1 cup salsa

1 package reduced sodium taco seasoning

1 can reduced fat cream of mushroom soup

1/2 cup reduced fat sour cream

Directions:

-Add Chicken to slow cooker

-Sprinkle with taco seasoning over chicken

-Pour salsa and soup over chicken

-Cook on low 6-8 hrs

-Remove from heat & stir in sour cream

Number of Servings: 6

Total Carbs: 11g

Low Carb Turkey Chili

Ingredients:

1 package lean ground turkey
1 onion
1 red bell pepper
2 cloves garlic
2 jalapenos
chili powder
ground cumin
ground coriander
dried oregano leaves
dried marjoram leaves
cinnamon
can of chopped tomatoes
tomato paste
fresh cilantro

Directions:

-Spray Pam in a large pot and brown turkey, onion, bell pepper, garlic, jalapeno and all spices.

-Once the turkey is fully cooked add 1 and a half cans (14.5 oz) of any chopped tomatoes, and 1 6 oz can tomato paste.

-Turn the burner down and let simmer for about 5 minutes.

-Add cilantro and stir.

-You can top this with low fat or fat free cheese and sour cream.

Number of Servings: 6

Total Carbs: 13.8

Low-Carb Slow Cooker Pork Carnitas

Ingredients:

One pork tenderloin (approximately a pound, but go bigger if you can)

One can of diced tomatoes w/ chiles

1/2 cup of onions

2 cloves of garlic

2 teaspoon cumin

2 teaspoons red pepper flake

Bag of spinach (approximately 4 cups)

4 tablespoons of sour cream

Directions:

-Heat 3 tablespoons of olive oil in a deep skillet on medium heat.

-Cut off all visible fat on tenderloin, season w/ salt and pepper (and any other seasoning that you like).

-Sear tenderloin on all sides (depending on heat and size will take about 5-7 mins). You want a good crust on it.

-In the meantime, pour the can of tomatoes into the slow cooker, add your cumin and red pepper flake and hot sauce to the tomatoes. Crank the heat on the slow cooker to high

-Once the tenderloin is nice seared, take it out of the pan and put on a plate.

-Reduce the heat to low/medium and add garlic and onions.

-Using a good knife, cut the tenderloin into 4-6 equal pieces. The middle will the raw, this is ok.

-Toss the pork into the slow cooker and toss it around in the tomatoes.

-Once the onions and garlic are translucent, add to the slow cooker. Cover the slow cooker and cook for 3-4 hours.

-Serve with 1 cup of raw spinach (the pork will wilt it perfectly) and 1 tablespoon of sour cream.

Total Carbs: 7.3g

Low Carb BBQ Ribs w/ Sauce

Ingredients:

DRY RUB

1 tbsp kosher salt

1 tbsp paprika

1 tsp garlic powder

1 tsp onion powder

1 tsp dried oregano

1 tsp black pepper

1/8 to 1/4 tsp cayenne pepper, depending on how hot you like it

RIBS

1 rack pork spare ribs

1 cup water

½ cup Low Carb Chipotle Whiskey Barbecue Sauce

Directions:

Preheat oven to 425F.

For the dry rub, mix kosher salt, paprika, garlic powder, onion powder, oregano, pepper and cayenne together in a small bowl.

Rub all over both sides of ribs. Lay ribs in a large roasting pan (cut in half if you need to, to make them fit). Add water and cover tightly in tinfoil.

Bake 1 & 1/2 hours, until meat is very tender.

Preheat grill or broiler. Brush ribs with sugar-free barbecue sauce and grill or broil 6 to 8 minutes, watching carefully so that they don't burn.

Ribs with BBQ Sauce (6 servings): 5g of carbs and 1.55 g of fiber. Total NET CARBS = 3.45 g

Low-Carb Slow Cooker Chicken Fajitas

Ingredients:

1 lb boneless, skinless pastured chicken breasts
3 bell peppers (try for a mix of red, yellow, and/or green bell peppers)
1 large onion
3 tablespoons fajita seasoning
1/2 cup chicken broth (low-sodium preferred)

Directions:

-Slice the onions and peppers into 1/2" strips and place at the bottom of a slow cooker

-Add the chicken breasts and sprinkle the Fajita seasoning on top.

-Add the broth and cook on low for 4-6 hours or until cooked through.

-Shred the chicken and serve the fajitas in lettuce wraps with a splash of lime juice on top (optional)

Total Carbs: 11.2g

Low-Carb Slow Cooker Chicken Alfredo

Ingredients:

1 lb grilled chicken strips
1 cup yellow squash chopped
1 cup sweet onions chopped
1 cup broccoli chopped
1/4 cup parmesan cheese
1/4 cup ground almonds
1 teaspoon montreal seasoning
2 cups light alfredo sauce

Directions:

-Put chicken, squash, onions, and broccoli in the slow cooker and sprinkle the montreal seasoning over everything.

-Pour the alfredo sauce over all of it making sure to cover everything.

-Cook on high for 4 hours.

-After 4 hours put everything in a casserole dish and sprinkle with the parmesan and almonds.

-Bake at 400 F for 15 minutes.

Serving Size: Makes 8 Servings

Total Carbs: 7.9g

BBQ Pulled Pork Roast

Ingredients:

1 cup chopped celery

1 cup chopped onions

1 cup ketchup

1 cup barbecue sauce

1 cup water

2 tablespoons vinegar

2 tablespoons Worcestershire sauce

2 tablespoons brown sugar

1 teaspoon chili powder

1 teaspoon salt

1/2 teaspoon pepper

1/2 teaspoon garlic powder

3 lbs boneless pork roast

Directions:

-Combine all ingredients except roast in the slow cooker.

-Add the roast.

-Cover, cook on high for 6-7 hours.

-Remove the roast.

-Shred the meat, and return it to the sauce.

-If desired, thicken the sauce by simmering on the stovetop.

Servings: 12

Total Carbs: 12.3

Low-Carb Slow Cooker Pot Roast

Ingredients:

1 arm pot roast, about 3.5 lbs

3 carrots, chopped in large chunks

3 stalks celery, chopped in large chunks

1 box of beef stock (about 3 cups)

1 envelope onion soup mix

Directions:

-Line the slow cooker with a liner or spray with cooking spray.

-Lay vegetables in first on the bottom of the slow cooker.

-Lay roast on top of vegetables.

-In separate bowl, mix beef stock and soup mix. Pour the mixture over the top.

-Add water if more liquid is needed. Cook 8-10 hours in slow cooker.

Number of Servings: 12

Total Carbs: 2.4g

Low Carb Roast Beef

Ingredients:

1 chuck roast, 1.69 weight (also called English roast)

1 teaspoon extra virgin coconut oil or extra virgin olive oil

1 cup petite carrots

1 jar of sliced mushrooms, drained

3/4 cup mixed onion and celery

1 cup of beef stock

1.5 teaspoons of beef base

1 cup of filtered water, heated to boiling

1 envelope of lipton onion soup mix (dry)

1/2 teaspoon kosher salt (optional)

Dash of black pepper

Directions:

-Line slow cooker with liner or spray with pan spray for easy clean-up. Trim fat from roast. Heat 1 teaspoon of coconut or olive oil in a large skillet and sear the roast on both sides.

-Layer baby carrots, mushrooms, and mirepoix mix in bottom of slow cooker. Salt and pepper both sides of meat and place on top of vegetables. Sprinkle dry onion soup mix over meat.

-Dissolve 1 1/2 teaspoons of beef base in 1 cup of boiling water. Pour beef stock and beef base mixture over meat.

Cover and cook for 6 to 8 hours on low or 3 to 4 hours on high.

Number of Servings: 8

Total Carbs: 6.4g

Provencal Chicken and Beans

Ingredients:

24 oz boneless, skinless chicken breast
1 yellow bell pepper, diced
1 red bell pepper, diced
1 (16 oz) can cannellini beans, drained and rinsed
1 (14.5 oz) can petite diced tomatoes with basil and oregano or any style of canned tomatoes
1 dash salt
1 dash black pepper
2 teaspoons dried basil
1 teaspoon dried thyme

Directions:

-Place all ingredients into a slow cooker, stir and cover with lid

-Cook on low heat for 7 hours

Makes 6 one cup servings.

Total Carbs: 19.8g

Slow Cooker Mexican Chicken

Ingredients:

1 package boneless, skinless chicken

1 cup salsa'

1/2 packet taco seasoning

1/2 can condensed cream of mushroom soup

Cilantro

Directions:

Mix salsa, cilantro, and condensed soup in a small bowl. Place chicken in slow cooker and sprinkle half of the taco seasoning packet over it. Top with salsa mixture and cook on high for 4 hours.

Number of Servings: 4

Total Carbs: 8.9g

Low Carb Jambalaya

Ingredients:

1 cup chopped onion
1 cup chopped green bell pepper
1 cup chopped celery
2 cloves garlic -- chopped
28 ounces canned tomatoes -- undrained
2 cups smoked sausage -- chopped
1 tablespoon dried parsley
1/2 teaspoon dried thyme
1/2 teaspoon salt
1/4 teaspoon pepper
1/4 teaspoon Tabasco sauce
3/4 pound medium shrimp -- raw, peeled, devein

Directions:

-Add all ingredients except the shrimp into a 3-6 quart slow cooker.
-Cover & cook on low for 7-8 hours (or on high for 3-4 hours).

-Stir in cleaned shrimp, cover & cook on low for about 1 hour or until shrimp are pink & firm.

Number of Servings: 8

Total Carbs: 6.3g

Pork with Beans

Ingredients:

Spice rub:

1 tablespoon chili powder

1/2 teaspoon red pepper flakes

1/2 teaspoon kosher or sea salt

2 lbs pork shoulder, visible fat removed

3 cloves garlic, halved

1 cup chicken stock, low sodium

1 (14.5-ounce) can low-sodium diced tomatoes

2 (14.5-ounce) cans cannellini beans, drained and rinsed

2 cups escarole or kale, chopped

1/2 cup pepitas

Directions:

-Prepare the spice rub by combining the chili powder, red pepper and salt.

-Rub over the pork shoulder 1 hour before cooking or the night before.

-Refrigerate the meat until ready to cook.

-Place the pork in a slow cooker with the garlic.

-Pour the stock over the meat. Cook on low for 5-6 hours.

-Remove the lid and break up the meat into large chunks.

-Add the diced tomatoes, beans and kale. Cook for another hour.

-Before serving, toast the pepitas in a dry skillet.

-Serve the stew warm, topped with the pepitas.

Servings: 8

Total Carbs: 11.7g

Pork Roast or Chops

Ingredients:

1 large onion, sliced
32 organic baby carrots, full or sliced
2 1/2 lbs boneless pork roast or 8-5oz. chops
1 cup hot water
1/4 cup white sugar or sweetener
3 tablespoons red wine vinegar
2 tablespoons soy sauce
1 tablespoons organic ketchup
1/2 teaspoon black pepper
1/2 teaspoon salt
1/4 teaspoon garlic powder
1 dash hot pepper sauce, or to taste

Directions:

-Arrange onion slices evenly over the bottom of the slow cooker, and then place pork on top of the onion.

-In a bowl, mix together water, sugar, vinegar, soy sauce, ketchup, black pepper, salt, garlic powder, and hot sauce; pour over pork.

-Add baby carrots.

-Cover, and cook on low for 6 to 8 hours, or on high for 3 to 4 hours.

Number of Servings: 8

Total Carbs: 13.8

Rosemary and Olive Oil Slow Cooker Chicken

Ingredients:

8 cloves garlic, sliced

1 Tbsp dried rosemary, crumbled between your fingers

1/2 tsp kosher salt

1/2 tsp black pepper

3 Tbsp Extra Virgin Olive Oil

3 Tbsp white wine

2 Tbsp water

2 lbs skinless, boneless chicken breasts

cooking spray

Directions:

-Spray slow cooker with the cooking spray.

-Mix all ingredients except the chicken in the slow cooker. Mix well. -Add the chicken one piece at a time, making sure to turn each piece to cover.

-Cook on low for eight hours or high for four hours.

Number of Servings: 8 servings

Slow Cooker Lasagna

Ingredients:

1 pound ground beef, 96% lean

1/4 tsp red pepper flakes

2 tsp dried thyme

One 24-ounce jar low-sodium marinara sauce

One 3/4-pound eggplant, unpeeled, diced (2 cups)

15 ounces part-skim ricotta cheese

1 cup shredded Italian five-cheese blend

1/4 cup egg substitute (or 1 egg white)

1 tbsp chopped fresh parsley

6 no-boil lasagna noodles

Directions:

-In a skillet over moderate heat, brown the ground beef and drain any excess fat. Stir in red pepper flakes, thyme, tomato sauce, eggplant, and 1 1/4 cup water.

-In a mixing bowl, combine the ricotta, shredded cheese blend, egg substitute, and parsley.

- Coat the inside of the slow cooker with nonstick cooking spray. Place enough meat sauce in the slow cooker to cover the bottom. Top with 2 or 3 lasagna noodles (break them up as needed) to cover the meat sauce. Repeat layer.

-Top the second layer with all of the cheese mixture and finish with a top layer of the remaining meat sauce.

-Cover and set the slow cooker on low. Cook for 3 1/2 to 4 hours.

Please note that the cooking time should not exceed 4 hours. This is not an "all day" slow-cooker meal.

Number of Servings: 8

Total Carbs: 18.1

BREAD + BAKING

Low Carb Cheesecake

Ingredients:

3 (8 ounce) packages cream cheese

25 (1 g) packets Splenda sugar substitute

1 cup sour cream

3 eggs

1 teaspoon vanilla extract

Directions:

-Preheat Oven To 375 Degrees F.

-Soften cream cheese in a large bowl. (Or microwave on defrost for 5 minutes.).

-With an electric mixer, blend cream cheese until creamy for one minute.

-Add sugar, eggs, vanilla and sour cream and blend until incorporated.

-Spray a 9' Round cake pan with Pam cooking Spray to prevent sticking.

-Add Batter to cake pan.

-Bake in oven for 45 minutes or until somewhat firm in the center. It will be brown and cracked around the edges. A true New York style cheese cake. If you do not want it to get real brown about halfway through the baking process put a tent of aluminum foil over it but make sure it does not touch top of cheese cake.

You can substitute whipped non sugared whipping cream that you made yourself without sugar instead of the sour cream.

Total Net Carbs: 5g per serving

Pumpkin Pound Cake

Ingredients

1 cup canned pumpkin

1 cup granulated Splenda or equivalent liquid Splenda

1 teaspoon baking powder

1 teaspoon vanilla

1/2 teaspoon pumpkin pie spice or 1 teaspoon cinnamon

Pinch to 1/8 teaspoon salt

5 eggs

6 ounces almond flour, about 1 1/2 cups

Directions

-Grease an 8x4" loaf pan well or line with foil and grease foil. In a medium bowl, beat the pumpkin, Splenda, baking powder, vanilla, spice and salt, if using, with an electric mixer until well blended.

-Beat in the eggs, then the almond flour. Add a little water, if needed, to make a thick, but pourable batter.

-Pour into the pan and bake at 300º 60-75 minutes, until the cake pulls away from the sides of the pan a bit and a toothpick comes out clean.

-Let cool in the pan on a rack for 10 minutes. Remove from the pan and peel off the foil; cool completely on a rack before slicing. Store in the refrigerator or freeze.

Total Net Carbs: 7g per slice

Lemon Pound Cake

Ingredients:

1/3 cup coconut flour

2/3 cup almond flour

¼ teaspoon sea salt

1 tablespoon glucomannan powder (optional, but improves texture & fiber)

Sweetener to equal 3/4 cup of sugar

6 drops liquid Splenda

3 tablespoons coconut oil

1 stick unsalted butter

½ teaspoon vanilla

Juice of 1 lemon

Zest of 1 lemon

8 large eggs, beaten

Directions:

-Preheat oven to 350º. Melt butter and coconut oil in microwave in a medium mixing bowl. Add almond flour, coconut flour, salt and glucomannan powder to the melted butter and oil and beat with a spoon until smooth.

-Add vanilla, zest and lemon juice. Add sweeteners. Add eggs. Beat with spoon until all lumps are out of batter. Using a rubber spatula, scrape the batter evenly into a lightly oiled non-stick loaf pan.

-Level batter as best you can with the spatula. Pop into preheated oven for 40-45 minutes or until it is lightly browned on top and passes the toothpick test in the center. Remove and cool before attempting to remove from pan and slicing. Enjoy plain or with a thin frosting on top.

Total Net Carbs: 3.5g

Carrot Cake

Ingredients

4 egg whites

12 packets of Truvia, or 1/2 cup equivalent

1/4 cup LC-Sweet Brown

1/4 cup Swerve

1/4 cup Greek Yogurt

3 tablespoons coconut oil -- melted, or softened

1 teaspoon vanilla

1/2 teaspoon orange extract

2 cups almond flour

2 teaspoon baking powder

1 teaspoon cinnamon

1/2 teaspoon ginger

1/2 teaspoon nutmeg

1/4 teaspoon salt

1 cup carrots -- shredded

1/4 cup hot water

Directions:

-Preheat oven to 350F. Grease 8 x 8-inch pan.

-In large bowl, add egg whites, Truvia, LC Sweet Brown, Swerve, Greek Yogurt, coconut oil, vanilla, and orange extract. With electric mixer beat until smooth and well blended.

-Add almond flour, baking powder, cinnamon, ginger, nutmeg, and salt. Beat on low speed until well combined. Add carrots and hot water and continue mixing until well blended.

-Pour into pan. Bake about 40 to 50 minutes or until toothpick comes out clean. Cool and frost with Coconut Rum Cream Cheese Frosting (below).

Coconut Rum Cream Cheese Frosting

Ingredients:

3 ounces philadelphia 1/3 less fat cream cheese -- softened

3 tablespoons butter -- softened

1/3 cup powdered sugar substitute

1/2 teaspoon rum extract

1/3 cup unsweetened shredded coconut

2 tablespoons coconut milk -- or cream--just enough for consistency

Directions:

-In medium bowl, combine cream cheese, butter, powdered sugar substitute, and rum extract.

-Beat until smooth and creamy.

-Add shredded coconut and coconut milk or cream, until it is a spreadable consistency, beating until smooth.

Total Net Carbs: 4g

Low Carb Paleo Chocolate Chip Cookies

Ingredients:

2 cups blanched almond flour

¼ teaspoon celtic sea salt

½ teaspoon baking soda

¼ cup palm shortening

2 tablespoons honey

1 tablespoon vanilla extract

½ cup chocolate chunks

Directions:

-Combine almond flour, salt and baking soda in a food processor

-Pulse in shortening, honey and vanilla until dough forms

-Remove blade from processor and stir in chocolate chunks by hand

-Scoop dough one level tablespoon at a time onto a parchment lined baking sheet

-Press balls of dough down gently

-Bake at 350° for 6-8 minutes

-Cool for 15 minutes (do not handle prior or cookies will break)

-Serve

Total Net Carbs: 4g

Peanut Butter Cookies

Ingredients

1/2 cup natural peanut butter

1/3 cup erythritol + 1 tablespoon garnish

1/3 cup coconut flour

1/4 cup flaxseed meal

5 tablespoons salted butter

1 large egg

1 tablespoon heavy whipping cream

1 teaspoon baking powder

1/4 teaspoom baking soda

Directions

-Preheat oven to 350F.

-In a mixing bowl, add softened butter and peanut butter.

-Add heavy cream and mix thoroughly.

-Add flax seed and coconut flour. You can add additional spices here if you'd like to have a different flavor.

-Mix the batter well until it becomes a bit thick and dough-like.

-Add your baking soda, baking powder, and erythritol and stir in very well. As you stir vigorously, the residual heat from the friction will start to warm the peanut butter.

-Add your egg to the mixture.

-Continue mixing very well until you get a creamy, but still pliable mixture.

-Roll your cookie dough into balls and place them on a cookie sheet. Make sure they are spread apart at least 1 inch on each side.

-Press each cookie down with your finger

-Bake them for 15 minutes. You want semi-crisp edges here. When you take them out of the oven they will feel extremely soft to the touch, but you need to let them completely cool. Once they come back to room temperature, they will start to harden up a little bit so they can be moved around easily.

-As they are cooling, sprinkle the top with Erythritol.

Total Net Carbs: 1.5g

Low Carb Sugar Cookies

Ingredients:

1 1/4 cups almond flour

1/2 cup Splenda

2/3 cup erythritol

1 egg

1/2 teaspoon butter flavored extract

1 teaspoon vanilla extract

1/4 cup unsalted butter, softened

Diabetisweet or granulated maltitol, or erythritol

Directions:

-Preheat oven to 350°F.

-Mix almond flour with Splenda and erythritol, sifting until well mixed. In a separate bowl, lightly beat egg and then mix well with extracts and softened butter. Add to dry ingredients and mix really well.

-Form dough into 24 small balls and space evenly on two ungreased cookie sheets (most cookie sheets will hold 12 cookies — 4 rows of three — very evenly.) Press moderately to flatten to a silver-dollar pancake size.

-Sprinkle cookies with granulated Diabetisweet or granulated Maltitol, or Erythritol, just as you would traditional "sugar" cookies. Bake for approximately 8 minutes at 350°F. They will slide right off the cookie sheet. Cool 5 minutes before eating.

Total Net Carbs: 3g

Oatmeal Cookies

Ingredients:

1 cup butter, at room temperature

1 ½ cups sugar substitute

1 tablespoon molasses

1 teaspoon pumpkin pie spice

2 eggs

1 cup almonds, ground

¼ cup oat bran

1 cup vanilla protein powder

1 teaspoon baking soda

1 teaspoon salt

2 cups oats

2 tablespoons flax seed meal

1 cup raisins

Directions:

-Mix together butter, Splenda, molasses and spice until creamy.

-Add eggs and beat until smooth.

-In a separate bowl mix together ground almonds, oat bran, baking soda, salt, flaxseed meal and oatmeal.

-Add slowly to butter mix and blend well.

-Add raisins and mix again.

-Preheat oven to 350 degrees.

-Spray 2 cookie sheets with cooking spray and drop dough onto them.

-These cookies do not spread out very much so you may want to press them down a little bit.

-Bake 8-10 minutes.

Total Net Carbs: 2g

Low Carb Irish Lace Cookies

Ingredients:

1/2 cup boiling water

4 packets Splenda

2 cups rolled oats

1 tablespoon unsalted butter

2 extra large eggs

1 teaspoon vanilla extract

2 teaspoons baking powder

1/2 teaspoon salt

Directions:

-Preheat oven to 350°F.

-Pour boiling water over the oats. Mix, cover, and set aside to soak. Meanwhile, beat the butter, sweetener, eggs and vanilla together until fluffy and smooth. Add baking powder and salt to the oats; then pour the oats into the creamed mixture and combine well.

-Drop by teaspoonful 2-3 inches apart on a greased cookie sheet. Bake 12-15 minutes and cool completely on rack. Store in an airtight container - layers separated by waxed paper or paper towels.

Total Net Carbs: 4g

Low Carb Lemon Butter Cookies

Ingredients:

1/2 cup butter, softened

1/3 cup granular Splenda or equivalent liquid Splenda

1 teaspoon lemon extract

1 teaspoon vanilla

1 teaspoon lemon zest, from 1 small lemon (1 gram)

1 egg

1 cup almond flour (4 ounces)

1/3 cup vanilla whey protein powder

1 teaspoon baking powder

Directions:

-Put everything in a medium bowl and beat with an electric mixer until creamy. This will only take about a minute.

-Using a 2 teaspoon cookie scoop, scoop 24 balls of the dough onto a silicone or parchment-lined baking sheet. Place them 6 balls across and 4 balls down on the sheet. Cover the dough balls with a sheet of wax paper. Very gently press them down with the bottom of a glass or small bowl to about 1/4-inch thick.

-Carefully remove the wax paper (the dough might stick to it a bit) and bake them at 350º about 8-12 minutes or until golden brown. Cool on a wire rack.

Number of Servings: 24

Total Net Carbs: 1g

Low Carb Gingersnaps

Ingredients:

3 ounces almond flour (3/4 cup)

1/4 teaspoon cinnamon

1/8 teaspoon ginger

1/8 teaspoon cloves

Pinch nutmeg

Pinch allspice

1/8 teaspoon salt

1 egg white

4 teaspoons granular Splenda or equivalent liquid Splenda

1/4 teaspoon blackstrap molasses

1/8 teaspoon vanilla

Directions:

-In a small bowl, blend the spices and salt with the almond flour. Stir in the remaining ingredients until well blended and a sticky dough forms. Drop the dough by teaspoons in 24 tiny piles on parchment-lined 12x17" baking sheet. Very lightly and gently pick up each piece of dough and roll into a ball; put back on the baking sheet making sure to space them evenly 6 across and 4 down.

-Cover the balls with plastic wrap and take a baking powder can, that has about an 1/8" rim around the bottom, and press down firmly over each ball of dough. Be sure to press all the way down to the baking sheet. Peel off the plastic wrap and repeat until all the cookies have been shaped.

-Prick them with a fork. You may have to gently hold the cookies down with one hand while pricking so that the dough stays put. Bake at 325º for 15-20 minutes or until golden brown. Remove from the pan and cool on a rack.

Total Net Carbs: 1g

Apple Cake

Ingredients:

1 6-ounce McIntosh apple

1/2 cup butter, softened

4 ounces cream cheese, softened

1 cup granular Splenda or equivalent liquid Splenda

5 eggs, room temperature

1 teaspoon vanilla

6 1/2 ounces almond flour, 1 1/2 cups plus 2 tablespoons

1 teaspoon baking powder

1 1/2 teaspoons cinnamon

Pinch salt

Directions:

-Peel and core the apple then chop finely.

-In a medium bowl, cream the butter, cream cheese and Splenda. Add the eggs, one at a time; blend in the extract. Mix the almond flour, baking powder, cinnamon and salt; add to the egg mixture a little at a time. Gently fold in the apples.

-Pour into a greased 8x8-inch cake pan. Bake at 350º 35-40 minutes. Its suggested to check the cake after 35 minutes. The cake will be golden brown and firm to the touch when done.

Total Net Carbs: 7g

Flourless Low Carb Chocolate Fudge Cake

Ingredients:

1/2 cup water

1/4 teaspoon salt

1 cup Splenda

1/2 cup erythritol

8 ounces unsweetened chocolate

1 cup unsalted butter

6 eggs

boiling water

Directions:

-Preheat oven to 300°F. Grease one 10 inch round cake pan and set aside.

-In a small saucepan over medium heat, combine the water, salt, Splenda and erythritol. Stir until completely dissolved and set aside.

-Either in the top half of a double boiler or in microwave, melt the chocolate. Pour the chocolate into the bowl of an electric mixer.

-Cut the butter into pieces and beat the butter into the chocolate — one piece at a time. Beat in the sweetened water. Slowly beat in the eggs — one at a time. Pour the batter into the prepared pan. Have a pan larger than the cake pan ready, put the cake pan in the larger pan and fill the pan with boiling water halfway up the sides of the cake pan.

-Bake cake in the water bath at 300°F for 45 minutes. The center will still look wet. Chill cake overnight in the pan. To unmold, dip the bottom of the cake pan in hot water for 10 seconds and invert onto a serving plate.

Total Net Carbs: 4.1g

Low Carb Coconut Cake

Ingredients:

1 cup egg whites – (from approximately 8 eggs)

1 tablespoon not/Sugar

12 packets Splenda

1/4 cup almond flour

1 3/4 cup unsweetened shredded coconut

1 teaspoon vanilla extract

Directions:

-Preheat oven to 350°F.

-Beat egg whites with not/Sugar, sweetener and vanilla until stiff. Fold in remaining ingredients as gently as possible.

-Place in preheated oven, turn off heat and bake overnight. (Note: ovens vary in the rate at which they lose heat — or whether you peek — so, if it comes out too moist, give it more time at no more than 300°F and next time, allow it to bake for a few minutes before turning off the oven.) If you are short on time, bake at 300°F until firm.

-Keep cake under refrigeration

Total Net Carbs: 2.4g

Mini Chocolate Cheesecakes

Ingredients:

1/4 cup semisweet or bittersweet chocolate chips, melted

1/2 cup part-skim ricotta

12 chocolate wafer cookies

1 tablespoon 100% fruit jam, such as raspberry or cherry

Directions:

-Combine melted chocolate and ricotta in a small bowl.

-Spoon a scant 1 tablespoon of the mixture on each chocolate wafer and top with 1/4 teaspoon jam.

Total Net Carbs: 8g

Low Carb Cheesecake Mousse

Ingredients:

8 ounces cream cheese, softened

1 cup heavy cream

1 (1/3 ounce) box sugar-free jello

$\frac{1}{2}$ cup boiling water

Directions:

-Melt sugar free jello (any flavor) in boiling water.

-Stir well to dissolve and cool slightly.

-Beat softened cream cheese until smooth and stir in cooled jello.

-Lightly fold in heavy cream until well mixed.

-Pour into serving dishes and put in fridge to chill at least 3 hours.

Total Net Carbs: 7.1g

Low Carb No Bake Cherry Cheesecake

Ingredients:

12 ounces cream cheese, allow to soften at room temperature at least 1 hour

2 packets different sugar substitutes (recommended 1 Splenda and 1 Equal for best flavor.)

1 teaspoon vanilla extract

1 cup heavy cream

1 cup no sugar added cherry pie filling.

Directions:

-Beat heavy cream in a bowl until it forms soft peaks. In a different bowl, using electric beater, combine softened cream cheese, sugar substitute, and vanilla.

-Beat whipped cream into the cream cheese mixture, using low speed of electric mixer. Transfer mixture to 6-8 individual small ramekins or glass dishes and chill at least one hour.

-This will keep in the refrigerator for several days.

Total Net Carbs: 7.2g

Low Carb No-Bake Raspberry Cheesecake

Ingredients:

1 8 oz package cream cheese, softened

1 tablespoon vanilla extract

1/2 cup heavy cream

1 tablespoon sugar-free raspberry syrup

Directions:

-Combine cream cheese and vanilla until well mixed and smooth.

-Whip cream and flavored syrup together, until whipped cream forms. (An immersion blender works well for this, but you can also do it with a hand-mixer or a wooden spoon.)

-Fold whipped cream into cream cheese mixture.

-Place in dish and refrigerate overnight.

Total Net Carbs: 2.7g

Low Carb Pumpkin Cheesecake Muffins

Ingredients:

1 package cream cheese

1 small can pure pumpkin

4 eggs

2 tablespoon ground flax seed

1 tablespoon brown sugar

1 teaspoon stevia plus

1 tablespoon pumpkin pie spices

1 tablespoon cinnamon, ground

1/2 teaspoon vanilla extract

Directions:

-Preheat oven to 375 degrees.

-Mix softened cream cheese, brown sugar, stevia and pumpkin until well mixed.

-Add spices, then mix well for several minutes.

-Pour into greased muffins tins.

-Bake for about 25 mins. Check for doneness.

Total Net Carbs: 3.4g

Coconut Cheesecake

Ingredients:

4 8-oz packages of cream cheese

1 cup Splenda sugar substitute for baking

1 6-oz light vanilla yogurt

2 tablespoons baking cocoa

1/2 cup unsweetened grated coconut

3/4 cup egg whites or egg substitute

1/2 cup Kashi Go Lean cereal

Directions:

Preheat oven to 325 degrees F.

Lightly coat the inside of a 9" springform pan with cooking spray (canola oil).

Crush cereal and sprinkle evenly over the bottom of the springform pan.

In a large bowl, mix cream cheese, Splenda and yogurt on medium speed.

Add egg whites, mix on low speed until blended.

Split batter into two bowls.

Fold coconut into the first bowl of batter. Transfer mixed batter to the springform pan, and spread across the bottom.

Mix cocoa into the second bowl of batter; spread cocoa batter over the first layer of batter in the springform pan.

Bake for 60-70 minutes, or until the middle is almost set.

Cool to room temperature, and then refrigerate for at least four hours.

Serve chilled.

Number of Servings: 12

Total Net Carbs: 10.5g

Low-Carb Cheesecake Balls

Ingredients:

1.5 oz. cream cheese

2 teaspoons sugar-free raspberry flavored jello

1 1/2 tablespoon hot water

1 teaspoon erythritol

1 1/2 teaspoon unsweetened cocoa

Directions:

-Dissolve jelly crystals in hot water and beat into cream cheese with erythritol and unsweetened cocoa. Refrigerate mixture until firm.

-Slightly dampen hands and pinch off a marble sized piece of the cheese mixture and roll into a ball.

-Do this with the rest of the cheese. Freeze for 30 minutes in a single layer on wax paper.

-Mix some extra cocoa and sweetener. Place in a gallon sized zipper bag and add frozen cream cheese balls. Shake gently to coat. Store in refrigerator in a single layer to prevent sticking.

Total Net Carbs: 1g per ball

71050065R00071

Made in the USA
Middletown, DE
19 April 2018